THE LEAP
OF FAITH

Other best-selling titles by
Dr. Paul Yonggi Cho:

The Fourth Dimension, Volume One

The Fourth Dimension, Volume Two
(with R. Whitney Manzano, PhD)

Solving Life's Problems

Successful Home Cell Groups
(with Harold Hostetler)

The authorized biography of
Dr. Paul Yonggi Cho:

Dream Your Way to Success
by Nell Kennedy

THE LEAP OF FAITH

DR· PAUL YONGGI CHO

author of
The Fourth Dimension

Bridge Publishing, Inc.
Publishers of:
LOGOS • HAVEN • OPEN SCROLL

Formerly titled *Discoveries in the Word*

The Leap of Faith

Copyright © 1984 by Bridge Publishing, Inc.
All rights reserved
Printed in the United States of America
Library of Congress Catalog Card Number:
International Standard Book Number: 0-88270-574-1
Bridge Publishing, Inc., South Plainfield, NJ 07080

Contents

This book of sermons is dedicated to all of my dear friends and partners. It is with total trust and faith in Jesus Christ the King of Glory that I have compiled this book to help bring people closer to Jesus.

Paul Yonggi Cho, D.D., D. Litt.

Foreword

Having traveled to Seoul, Korea, and experienced worship at the Full Gospel Yoido Church, now numbering 400,000 members, I know the importance of Dr. Cho's gifted preaching ability. This aspect of his ministry has a significant role in the unusual growth of "the world's largest church." My first visit was in February, during the bitter, cold winter season Koreans must endure. I remember how impressed I was to see thousands of faithful believers waiting in such long lines to get a seat inside the church. Men in business suits, little children bundled and held close by their mothers, all patiently waited with anticipation.

"What causes them to brave the weather and wait in such long lines?" I asked Dr. Cho during one of his twenty-minute breaks between the seven regular Sunday services.

His answer caused me to see the need for this book of prophetic messages.

"These people are hungry for a message from God," Dr. Cho answered. "I share with them messages which minister to their need. My topics are current and relevant. This is why they come."

I believe Dr. Cho's message in this book will inspire anyone, from any country or cultural background. His topics are just as timely and important for those of us in the western world as they are for Koreans.

May the Holy Spirit bring His understanding to your heart as you read this book.

R. Whitney Manzano, Ph.D.
Consultant to Dr. Cho

Introduction

As of this summer, our church has gone past the 300,000 membership goal I set two years ago. The greatest problem we have in our church at this time is space, not only for our present congregation, but also for all of the new converts. We seat 30,000 people a service in our main auditorium and in our many chapels which are tied in by closed circuit television. With seven services, we only have room for 210,000 people on Sunday. That means that not everyone in our membership can come to church every Sunday. Thank God for the Cell System!

We have approximately 20,000 cells in our church. These individual units comprise the practical ministry of our membership. Each cell is led by a trained leader who cares for no more than fifteen families. When the cell gets too large, they divide into two cells. The problem of division is that people don't want to be separated. However, every leader trains an assistant so that the divisions run as smooth as possible. These 20,000 cells care and nourish the members of our church.

Our goal is a membership of 500,000 members in our local church by 1984. We are presently constructing a new church building which will seat 25,000 people. This new building, in conjunction with the new chapel, will be able to accommodate 55,000 people a service. By continuing to have seven services each Sunday, we will be able to house a total of 385,000. So you can see the problem I have, particularly when you realize that we are winning people to Christ at the rate of 12,000 converts per month.

Why do so many people want to come to a church that is already crowded? Why do they stand in line for over one hour before each one of our seven services just to get a seat. The answer is that our Christians are hungry for the Word of God.

With seven services on Sunday, our services cannot last more than one and one half hours. Although we have a full symphony orchestra and wonderfully

Introduction

trained musicians, our people love to sing the praises of God, and we spend time praying together (actually most of our praying is done on Wednesday night; Friday, all night; and at Prayer Mountain), we spend most of the time in the Word of God. I have to wait upon the Lord for my messages. The Holy Spirit speaks to me; I pray and study and present the Word of the Lord to the people. Since not everyone can get to the services, my messages are reprinted and passed along to the cell group leaders. They are also video taped and shown in several countries.

These messages that I preach to my church have been enclosed in this book with the prayer that you also might be blessed. If you have any questions or comments, please write me in care of: Bridge Publishing, Inc., 2500 Hamilton Blvd., South Plainfield, NJ 07080.

My prayer for you is that the Holy Spirit will draw you closer to the Lord and Savior Jesus Christ through these *Leaps of Faith*.

1
Man's Three Great Discoveries

We are living in an age which is deluged with new inventions, called by some the Computer Age. We also see in our newspapers and magazines new discoveries which affect our lives. In the area of medicine, cures are being discovered to solve many of our physical problems, yet men are still sick. Scientifically, we have learned about the smallest and largest areas of our existence. Physicists are studying the world of the atom and the particles which make up the atom, and Astronomers are learning more about the vast universe in which we live. Yet with every new discovery, more new questions are raised than the ones which are answered.

Today, I want to share with you the real discoveries basic to man's existence here in this world and in the world to come.

MAN'S NEED

One of the most troubling things in our society today is that man knows he has a need, but does not know what it is. People are trying to fill the void that is within them with many different things. In trying to fill this void, man has thought that by becoming free of his inhibitions and restrictions, he would become happy.

In desiring to be free from moral restrictions, man has become a slave to immorality. In a recent study taken in California, the trendsetting state in the United States, many college students were asked about their sex life. A surprising eighty percent of those polled, both men and women, thought that their sex life was unsatisfying. Although they had experimented freely, they have now become bored with sex. In fact, a growing number of young people now feel that it is best to wait until after the commitment of marriage before having sex. This is not new to Christians. God in His Word teaches that sex is to be kept only within the sanctity of marriage. Yet, what is new is that many non-Christian young people are learning the hard way what the Holy Spirit revealed two thousand years ago in the Scriptures.

Having come through one of the darkest times of our century during the Depression forty years ago, many parents have tried to give their children things which they themselves were not able to have materially. Today, we take for granted the prosperity which is ours. With more leisure time and money, people have tried to buy happiness; yet the void remains. Have you ever been a little depressed and gone shopping to try to relieve your depression? Some women feel that by buying a new hat or a new pair of shoes, they will be able to satisfy themselves. But it does not work. Men also do the same thing by buying a new automobile or a new gadget. Yet their void remains. The answer to the void does not lie in material possessions, the answer lies within our hearts.

Lost humanity is like a child walking in the forest. He is dressed in nice clothing and has his pockets full of candy. It is a lovely summer day and the sky is blue. He enjoys walking on the softly padded paths and can only think of how good it feels to be alive. Yet when the sun begins to go down, he realizes that he has lost his way and does not know how to get back home. Suddenly, the candy in his pocket and the nice clothes on his back are of little interest to him. He is lost! While everything seemed to be going well, he was not concerned about his path; but now that it is too late, he realizes his foolishness. Today's man is very similar to this child.

THE WAY OUT

What do we have to do to find our way home? What can satisfy that void within us that we all feel? To answer these two important questions, we must look at God's Holy Word. His Word has the principles that will guide us back to the safety of our heavenly Father.

Take your Bible and look with me at Genesis, chapter one. If we desire to go home, we first must know where home is. In order for us to look for our home, we must first know about our original home and purpose. "And God said, Let us make man in our image, after our likeness; and let them have dominion over the fish of the sea, and over the fowl of the air, and over the cattle and over all the earth, and over every creeping thing that creepeth upon the earth. So God created man in his own image, in the image of God created He him, male and female created He them" (Gen. 1:26, 27). In Genesis, chapter two, we see God created man, not a second time, but from a different perspective: "And the Lord God formed man of the dust of the ground and breathed into his nostrils the breath of life; and man became a living soul. And the Lord God planted a garden eastward in Eden; and there he put the man whom he had formed" (Gen. 2:7, 8).

In chapter one God shows the creation of man within a cosmological perspective: Man is created as the focal point of the creation of the entire universe. He also gives man a purpose. Man's purpose is dominion, not over other men, but dominion beginning in the sky, the earth and finally, over those creatures that crawl over the earth. In the second chapter, God shows man's creation in a more personal and intimate way. While the other creatures were created by His speaking them into existence, man is not just spoken into existence, he is formed by God's own hand. God shows extreme personal attention by forming man from the earth and then breathing life into him, giving him a soul. God took the lowest—earth from the ground —and mixed it with the highest—His divine breath—in creating man. God also placed man within an ideal environment: The Garden of Eden. So what happened? Man sinned. He took the great gift God had given him, that is his free will, and used it to destroy his environment, purpose and goal.

However, he is still God's creature, having all of the desires of the original purpose; yet he cannot enjoy the blessings that he was created for because of the problem of sin. Try as he will to get back to the Garden in his heart, he is unable to cross the great barrier of sin which he has by his own disobedience created. Although we know where His home is located, the question still remains: How does he get back? Is the path lost forever? No! God has created a way back. He has not allowed man to wander back on his own. God has paid a dear price to create a path back to Himself—Jesus Christ.

Although the path was costly, it was crucial for the survival of God's most prized creations. The construction work was completed when Jesus said, "It is finished!" Now man does not have to live his life lost in the forest of sin and unfulfillment. By accepting the redemptive work of Christ, man can be salvaged and brought home and he is capable of accomplishing the great goals that God has given him. This is the good news of the gospel.

Not only has Christ paid the price for us to be delivered from the original sin of Adam, but He has created a way in which the effects of that sin can also be eradicated. The negative force that caused man to disobey naturally has been neutralized by the blood that was shed on Calvary's hill outside Jerusalem almost two thousand years ago. Through Christ, man can be a new creature and have his past dealt with effectively and have his future secured positively.

MAN'S ANSWER

Paul reveals this answer in his two letters to the church at Corinth: "Therefore, if any man be in Christ, he is a new creature; old things are passed away; behold, all things are become new" (2 Cor. 5:17). Also, "It is because of Him that you are in Christ Jesus, who has become for us wisdom from God, that is our righteousness, holiness and redemption" (1 Cor. 1:30).

All you have to do is read what is on the bookshelves of our bookstores today and you can easily see that man is not wise in himself. In trying to be wise, man has become foolish. One of the things that people who don't know Christ take for granted is the new theories of evolution. Although Darwin has been discredited by most scientists, they still feel that man has evolved over millions of years from smaller organisms.

Although the mathematical probabilities of a higher being evolving a smaller order by the laws of chance are almost nonexistent, men of science still cling to their random theories. In fact, it takes more faith to believe what is being taught today in our schools than to believe in the account of man's creation in Genesis.

The secular view of education has caused great havoc in not only our schools, but in our society in general.

Traditional moral values are being replaced by situational ethics. That is, anything is right as long as the situation warrants it. There are no absolute values, because this would have to have a God as the basis of those values. In search for freedom, society has been victimized by license.

The truth is that wisdom resides in Jesus Christ. This fact is not only true in science and education, but, it is also true in our political life as well. Plato, the Greek philosopher who wrote about democracy in his famous *Republic*, also stated that this system of self-government could not last over a long period of time. The observation has been made that when people realize that they can vote riches upon themselves by electing officials who make promises they cannot pay for, the whole democratic system would fall. Yet, in Christ we find freedom, but along with the freedom, we find restrictions. God not only promises us freedom, but then He tells us how to live. There can be no higher order for justifying laws than those laws coming from the Creator. As soon as a group of people try to bypass the Creator, those laws are then subject to review and will eventually be destroyed.

As we have seen, the only answer for a purposeful existence in this life is Jesus Christ. He gives us a reason for living. He gives us "peace that passeth all understanding." What does this mean? It simply means that sometimes things happen that are beyond our control. Life is not always peaceful. Tragedies do happen to good people. Yet the peace that Christ gives us transcends our understanding, because in the midst of the circumstance that peace and joy becomes even more peaceful. He is able to do that for you, if you will trust Him.

MAN'S POTENTIAL

As we read in Genesis, man has a great calling. He was created by God to rule over his surroundings. Yet this potential for ruling has to be guided and directed by his Creator. Although man has a potential for ruling, his potential without the rule of God is more dangerous than we realize.

Throughout his history man has been plagued by wars. The basis of war is man's desire not only to rule his surroundings, but also to rule other men. Only in Christ can man's dominion instincts be properly directed to God's purposes.

Man also has a potential to discover new things. He is by nature curious. This potential was manifested and revealed by God in Genesis the eleventh chapter. If you turn to this chapter, you will be able to see with me a remarkable aspect of man's potentiality.

"And the whole earth was of one language, and one speech. And they said, Go to, let us build us a city and a tower whose top may reach into heaven; and let us make us a name, lest we be scattered abroad upon the face of the whole earth" (Gen. 11:1, 4).

In these verses we read several important facts about man after the Fall and the Flood:

Man's Three Great Discoveries

1. Originally, men were all of one language.

Etymology is a very interesting science dealing with the tracing of words back to their original use. One of the most interesting aspects of this field is the fact that although there are so many languages, there are remarkable similarities between words, particularly regarding basic words dealing with relationships and feelings.

In studying words and their roots, we have learned that most languages are related. This proves that at one time all people must have had one language.

2. Man had a desire to reach up to God, but his desire was only natural and not spiritual.

By building a large tower, man desired to reach up with purely human means. He could have tried to reach God by praying to the God of their forefather Noah, but instead they tried to do it through bricks and mortar.

13

3. Man was concerned about staying together.

Man cannot live by and to himself; he is a social creature. His desires are also social. A person not only identifies himself as an individual, but he sees himself as a part of a family, a society and particularly, a group.

The most remarkable aspect of this story is God's reaction to man's effort: "And the Lord said, Behold, the people is one, and they have all one language; and this they begin to do; and now nothing will be restrained from them, which they have imagined to do" (Gen. 11:6).

Moses tells the story of what happened several generations after Noah saved his family from the flood. He was in direct contact with God, and God showed him what happened at the tower of Babel. Moses reveals in Genesis God's concern because of man's seemingly unlimited potential and capability to do all that was within his imagination and understanding.

OUR LIMITATION IS ONLY LIMITED TO OUR IMAGINATION

One of our greatest problems as humans is our self-image. We don't realize what a capable creation we are. God has created within us the potential for accomplishments that are still too great for us to understand. Even with the scientific and technological advancements of the past ten years, we have but scratched the surface of our capabilities.

God said of man, "Nothing will be restrained from them, which they have imagined to do." According to the Creator, man is only limited by his imagination.

The imagination is that part of man's mind that creates the pictures which give context to his actions. Neurologists have discovered that athletes must first have a mental picture before they are capable of performing athletic feats. Before an artist paints, he must have a mental picture; before an architect designs a building, he must first have a mental picture. All accomplishments that are creative in nature emanate first from a mental picture which is in the mind of the person.

The reason why people don't create new ideas is because they don't realize the mental aspect involved in creative thinking. They don't allow themselves to dream and envision. If we are able to dream and see visions of abstract things, then we are also able to imagine. By developing our imagination, we are then able to become creative.

The great hindrance to man's potential is in his separation. God created differences in language to keep man from accomplishing his imaginative potential. However, this is not the final word. When Christ died and was resurrected, He said that it was important for Him to go back to His Father so that the Holy Spirit would come. When the Holy Spirit came at the day of Pentecost, the sign that the Holy Spirit had arrived was the ability given to the disciples to speak in unknown languages. Yet in

Acts we see that before this happened, the disciples were all in one place and were in one accord.

As the confusion of languages at the Tower of Babel separated man, so also the unity of languages at Pentecost brought man together. Now that we have been given the Holy Spirit, our limits have been lifted and our imaginations have been freed to accomplish not what we naturally envision, but what the will of God directs us to do.

Finally, we can see the importance of finding the path that God has created for us from the bondages of human freedom. For the path leads to a great future of unlimited potential here in this world and in the world to come.

Are you lost in the forest? Have you forgotten the way home? If you come to Christ who is the way home to the Father, then you will find that the void within you can be filled. You will also see the great potential you have to accomplish the will of God for your life. You will be able to dream dreams and see visions. Your creative potential can be realized.

AMEN!

2
Egoism or Egotism?

Today I want to share with you a common problem with an uncommon solution. The common problem is self. Self is something which all of us have, but unfortunately all of us don't know what to do about it.

Before we analyze the problem, we should know the word which best describes it: *egoism*. However, many people are confused and call it *egotism*. What is the difference?

Egotism is a tendency to speak or write about ourselves excessively and boastfully. An egotist is usually conceited and boastful. He is normally considered to be selfish. Although this is a real problem, usually for people that have to deal with people like that, it is not what I wish to address.

Egoism is much broader and more complex. Egoism is a mode of thinking or acting with only oneself and one's self's interest as the prime concern. It is a preoccupation with our own welfare and advancement. It says, "Only think of number one." Ethically, it is the thinking that what is best is always what is best for me. It believes that what is best for us is a just and rational justification for all conduct. It is the great deceit of our age.

This portion of Scripture sounds like Paul has just finished reading today's newspaper, "This know also, that in the last days perilous times shall come. For men shall be lovers of their own selves, covetous, boasters, proud, blasphemers, disobedient to parents, unthankful, unholy, without natural affection, trucebreakers, false accusers, incontinent, fierce, despisers of those that are good, traitors, heady, highminded, lovers of pleasure more than lovers of God, having a form of godliness but denying the power thereof: from such turn away" (2 Tim. 3:1-5).

Popular songs on the radio today have essentially one important line: "If it feels good, do it!" This kind of hedonism is affecting our young people. The moral implications of our actions are not considered. The question of the ethics of something is not thought through before people act today. The music world tells them to act. If they want to do something, anything they want to do is permissible.

Albert Camus, the Swiss existentialist philosopher, believed that the only way we should show our existence was by acting. Bookstores are full of books showing us how we should not be concerned about our natural inhibitions, but we should learn how to act without restriction. Man has become imprisoned by trying to be free.

In the business world, men cannot conduct business without hiring a large number of attorneys. Contracts have to be written in such a way that every loophole has to be closed so that the other party cannot get out of doing what he promised to do. This symptom of our age shows the great rise of egoism in our socicty.

AN OLD STORY WITH A CONTEMPORARY MESSAGE

In Luke 15:11-24 Jesus told a story that has great meaning to us today: "A certain man had two sons: and the younger of them said to his father, Father, give me the portion of goods that falleth to me." Although this younger son was not fully grown into an adult, he already thought of the portion that would someday become his, and his only thoughts were, "Give me my share of the family estate."

I am sure that the father thought he would someday divide his estate between his two sons, but the younger one thought he knew better and wanted it now. He was acting in his own best interest. What if the father died prematurely and the older brother got everything? Perhaps, the family might have a financial crisis and the estate would have to be sold in order to pay off debts. Egoism always thinks of the now and does not worry about tomorrow. The most important thing in the mind of the younger brother was the need at hand. He needed and wanted to be on his own, yet he did not want to rely upon his own resources or the potential from his own labors. No. He was going to get what was coming to him now.

Egoism is not only for children, parents are also guilty of the same thing. Have you known of parents who force their children to go into schools that might be too difficult for their children's ability? Sometimes parents force children to choose professions that will only build up their own prestige without thinking of the child. I have known of mothers and fathers who try to get their child married into the "right family" without thinking of the welfare of the child involved. What kind of parent are you?

Relationships are often built out of a motivation of egoism. A young man who was studying to become a medical doctor met a young lady at a party. After talking to her for a while, he discovered that she came from a prosperous family. While not loving her, he pretended to be interested in marriage. Soon he was living in the home of the young lady and her parents. Her parents, wanting their daughter to marry a promising young and handsome doctor, supported the young man in school. After several years the man became a doctor and opened up a lucrative private practice. He then moved out of the house and broke up with the young lady who had waited patiently for him to complete his studies. Heartbroken, the girl was the victim of a young man who was an egoist and the misdirected ambitions of her parents who did not advise her properly.

THE PATH OF THE EGOIST

Christ told the story of the younger son as his life developed. *You see, a person who only thinks of himself is not building solid relationships which will last through the storms that life brings. The relationships that resulted from his stubborn and self-centered decision were only temporary: He was surrounded by prostitutes until his money ran out: Then he was rejected by his friends and left to starve like a beggar.*

The greatest investment you can make is not with money, but with yourself. If you give yourself unselfishly to others, eventually it returns to you with interest like bread upon the waters.

Many finds it easy to go up, but it is very difficult to come down. The young man had been accustomed to living in a lovely home with servants. His needs were provided for him by his loving father. But the prodigal son wanted to do "his thing." Now that famine had come into the land of his riotous living, he found himself living in a pig pen.

It is the same with today's society that does not see the need to accept Jesus Christ. With faith in Christ comes a new self-image and self-worth.

This causes people to become industrious and prosperous. God has allowed us to prosper as long as our prosperity comes from the fruit of our own labor. He has not created us to live like pigs, but has created us to live with dignity, because we are created in His divine image. Yet, I see young people today living in terrible surroundings. While in India I noticed two young American men dressed like the poor beggars of that country. As I looked at them in their pitiful surroundings, I wondered where they came from and how their arrived at this terrible place—a street in Calcutta. I found out they were both from good homes in America, but decided to come to India to learn about life. They could have learned much more by picking up their Bible.

We must remember that the egoist is excessively preoccupied with his own self-interest to the disinterest of others. This does not mean that we should not act in our self-interest. Acting this way is natural. God recognizes our motivation to act in our own interest when He presents His message. Malachi, the prophet, motivated Israel to be faithful to God by showing them what they will receive in return for their obedience. However, my concern is with excessive self-interest which leads to eventual disaster.

JESUS THE EXAMPLE TO FOLLOW

Jesus Christ not only died for our sins and rose from the dead, but He also lived a life as an example to follow. In Christ, God not only commanded man to live righteously, but He came down and gave an object lesson.

If we look at the prayer which has been named, "The Lord's Prayer," we see Christ in juxtaposition to the egoist. In His prayer, Christ says, "Our Father," not "my" Father; He is concerned for "our daily bread," not "my bread." By praying this way, Jesus Christ identified himself with the disciples that were learning how to pray. He was part of the group.

Here in South Korea we are surrounded by difficult circumstances threatening our democracy. We have the North Korean Communists at our northern border; we have the Chinese Communists and the Soviet Union, all in close proximity. There are millions of armed troops poised to attack our liberty and freedom, especially our freedom of worship. We understand what it is to be under the oppression of the Japanese before and during World War II. We were then attacked without provocation by the Communists and we saw our land devastated. We, above most people on this earth, need to have a sense of community. We cannot be just concerned about me and mine. Christ is the best example of how we can overcome the natural tendency to be selfish.

The egoist is only concerned about what he can get for himself. He always says, "Give me!" God, however, is always giving: "For God so loved the world that He *gave* His only begotten

Son . . ." (John 3:16). Paul in his second letter to the Corinthian church shows the ultimate sacrifice of Christ. He shows the willingness of Christ to become sin for us, who knew no sin, that we might be made the righteousness of God in Him. Jesus, who lived a perfect and sinless life, was willing to become the embodiment of sin at the Cross for you and me that, because of His sacrifice, we might be made as righteous as His Father.

That is the key to overcoming: the recognition of the sacrifice of Jesus Christ. Love has no greater action than the willingness to lay down your life for someone else. In this way, Christ has made the ultimate sacrifice to destroy man's most pernicious motivational force: egoism.

THE RIGHT DECISION

Fortunately, no one is beyond help in this world. All of us have hope. No matter what your circumstances may be, you can be set free by the Truth of the Word of God.

The prodigal son was in the mire and pit, but his mind was able to come to its senses. He said, "How many of my father's hired men have food to spare, and here I am starving to death. I will arise and go to my father, and I will say unto him, 'Father, I have sinned against heaven and before Thee'" (Luke 15:18).

Why is it that we have to wait until we are totally out of our personal resources to get us out of the mire before we turn to the source of help, our Heavenly Father? It seems that the human race only turns for help when they cannot help themselves. Yet, we must be grateful that the mind can eventually come to its senses. We can wake up and say, "I need help and I will go back to the Father."

Notice that the son seemed to be in a dream of self-deception before he woke up to the reality of his situation. Once he woke up, he was able to make two very important decisions.

Egoism or Egotism?

1. He needed help.

You will never find help if you don't believe you need it. The only sadder thing than having a problem is not to realize that you have that problem.

2. He would turn to the right source for help.

God has the answer to every one of your problems. He has the answer to your marital, family, financial and physical problems, but He is waiting for you to turn to Him. As long as you think you can do it on your own, He will wait. But once you turn to Him, He is in a position to help you.

THE RECEPTION

The young man came back to the father thinking that he was just going to be treated like one of the servants. To his surprise, the father planned a great feast and personally went out to meet him upon his return. He put on him a special robe signifying that he was a son and placed upon his finger the family ring. He was accepted back into the family without recrimination.

This is the kind of reception that is awaiting everyone that wakes up to the fact that they have made a mistake. Our Heavenly Father is a God of love. He is waiting with open arms for all those that will return to Him.

I am sure that the experience of forgiveness dramatically changed the young man's life. He would never turn to the world again. He would never turn to the philosophy of egoism again. He would follow the example of his father and learn to love.

Yes, love is the opposite of egoism. Love is the way of life that is willing to sacrifice for others. Love never looks solely at its own self-interest, but it is interested in the needs of others.

Men will be attracted to this loving Christ whom we serve if we love one another. In this country, we must show those that don't know Christ that we are right, not by our many words only,

Egoism or Egotism?

but by our actions. As we are concerned for one another's needs, as we help and minister to one another, the world will accept this Christ that has set us free, and they will be saved.

AMEN!

3

God's Name Is God's Answer

God is addressed in the Bible by several names. Names were very important in the Old Testament times because they signified the character of the individual. For example, Jacob, which means "supplanter," was given that name at his eighth day when he was circumcised. Yet the nature of that name became evident in his personality until he had a change of character. At that time, God changed his name from Jacob to Israel. Once we understand this fact, then we can study and understand that the names used for God are important in knowing His answer to all of our needs.

Charles Spurgeon, a great English preacher and author of the last century, had a very unusual conversion. He was just a small boy, but he decided he wanted to go to church one Sunday morning. On his way, he looked up at the sky and could see that this cold winter day would bring a snow storm, but he decided to continue. The snow then began to come down like a white blanket over the beautiful English countryside. It got so bad that the preacher of the small Methodist church could not make it to the service. However, an uneducated deacon got up to give the sermon. Due to his lack of preparation he was self-conscious, but he began his short message by saying, "Look unto me, and be ye saved, all the ends of the earth: For I am God, and there is none else."

Charles later remembered that he could not recall the message that was preached that eventful snowy Sunday, but he was struck by the Scripture quoted. His mind could not forget the command to look to God. It repeated over and over again in his mind until he decided to commit his life to God. Of course, we all know that Spurgeon

became one of the greatest preachers of
his day.

All of us need to look to God for our
answers. Every problem has a solution,
not in abstract logic, but in the living
God. Yet, what is this God like? How
can we look to someone we don't know?
Can we know this God of the Bible? The
answer is yes. We can know Him
because He has been revealed in His
own Word: the Scriptures.

JEHOVAH JIREH—
JEHOVAH PROVIDER

God meets all of us at the point of
need. In the life of Abraham, again and
again, He met him at the point of his
need. In the twenty-second chapter of
Genesis, we see the most crucial test of
Abraham's life.

Abraham had been obedient to God
when he left his home and traveled
without knowing where God was
sending him. He also waited for
twenty-five years before God's promise
of giving him a son through his wife

Sarah came to pass. He had been torn by having to send his first son, Ishmael, away with his mother, because he could not be a joint heir with his son of promise, Isaac. Now God had told him to sacrifice his son of promise on an altar at Mt. Moriah. How could he kill the son he had waited twenty-five years to have? Could God provide another son now that he was over one-hundred and twenty years old? This is the dilemma that faced Abraham as he climbed the mountain with sacrifice in hand to obey God's command.

On the way, his son asked Abraham, "Where is the sacrifice?" By the time his obedient son had asked the question, Abraham had the solution: he would trust the God who had never failed him. If God did not provide a sacrifice miraculously, then He could raise Isaac from the dead. It was this type of faith in the faithfulness of God that caused him to be called the Father of Faith.

When I think of Abraham's obedience, I relate to the torment he went through. I have three boys, whom I love very much. I can't imagine walking for three days to the pinnacle of a mountain to sacrifice any one of them. Yes, His grace is sufficient. God never asks us to do anything without the sufficient grace to obey.

After arriving at the top of the mountain, Abraham prepared the altar, laid the wood down and bound his son. As he placed him on the altar and was about to slay him with his knife, he heard a voice from heaven saying, "Abraham, Abraham, don't harm your son! Now I know that you are obedient to my command!"

As the voice from heaven faded, he heard the bleating of a lamb. As he turned, he saw a lamb caught in the thicket. He went and took the lamb and put it on the altar in place of his son Isaac. God had provided the sacrifice! Abraham then called upon JEHOVAH-JIREH.

God had provided in the nick of time. He had tested Abraham, but had made provision. God always makes provision, even before the need. Christ is called "the Lamb slain before the foundation of the earth." Before the earth was ever formed, before man ever sinned, before there was any need for sacrifice, God had provided. God knew He would provide for Abraham, but Abraham had to accept it by faith. That is, Abraham had to see the provision before it ever appeared. That total and complete confidence is the very essence of faith.

In 1964, I became engaged to my wife, Grace. At that time, I had absolutely nothing to give to her as an engagement present. Our custom is to give your fiancee a special gift; I told her that I would give to her a wristwatch. Then, I began to calculate my net assets: a few bits of clothing (all well-used), a few study books and a Bible. In other words, I had nothing to sell to buy the watch. I prayed and asked JEHOVAH-JIREH to provide me with a watch for my future wife; then I began to calculate how God could answer my prayer. The Bible says that God's ways are beyond finding out, but that does not keep us from trying to figure them out. God loves to provide for us out of His abundance; yet His provision is usually by means and sources that are beyond our comprehension. God has a "ways and means committee": when we ask Him to meet our needs, the committee figures and makes provision. But God has so many ways of meeting our needs. It seems that every time we try to figure out how God is going to answer our prayer, the "ways and means committee" crosses out that possibility and we are left still having to trust Him.

That Sunday I preached with a heavy anointing from the Holy Spirit. Surely someone would be especially blessed and would hand me the watch God had provided. But no, nothing like that took place. The last person left and I had nothing. At the end of the night service, I also waited for my provision, but still nothing. What could I do? Well, I decided I would wait at the church until someone came.

At that time, we had a twelve o'clock midnight curfew in Korea. No one could travel after midnight until morning, or they would be stopped by the police. I looked at the time in the church and saw that the hour was getting very close to midnight. I again prayed, "Father, you were JEHOVAH-JIREH to Abraham; I know you are the great provider. Won't you be my provider?" The answer came to my heart, "Yes, I am your provider, too!" With that, peace came to my heart. I knew that God had the answer and had made provision. I was going to trust His Word, yet my mind was paying attention to the clock on the wall. Within a few minutes, the curfew would be in effect and no one would be able to come to the church and bring my watch.

Just before the midnight hour came, a knock came to our church door. My heart stopped as I wondered whether this was God's provision. I opened the door, and before me was an American gentleman in his pajamas. This man had been a soldier with the United States armed forces during the Korean War. He had been wounded, but had decided to stay in our country. He also attended our church. Although the wound had left him rather eccentric, he was a lovely Christian who really served God faithfully.

"What are you doing here at this time of night, brother," I asked him, seeing the look of perplexity on his face.

"Pastor Cho, I have a real problem," he answered me as he walked in the opened door.

Determined to get him out before he would have to spend the night at the church, I said, "Sir, if you think you have a problem, you don't know the problem I have. You had better go home right away before the beginning of the curfew and I will speak to you tomorrow!"

"No, pastor. Only you can solve my problem," he responded.

As the man walked towards my office, my only thoughts were on what I would tell Grace in the morning. I had promised my future wife that I would give her our engagement gift on Monday morning. What would I tell her? How could I expect her to marry me after I did not keep my promise?

"Boy, what a mess I have gotten myself into," I thought as I sat down and tried to pay attention to what this American was going to share with me.

As he sat down, he looked at me and I could see the worried look on his face. I then figured that he had a real problem so I had better listen to him. However, my thoughts were on the look on Grace's face if I arrived in the morning without an engagement gift.

"Pastor Cho, I have a niece back home in America. Next week is her birthday. You know I love my family and so I tried to buy something for her that she would really enjoy."

"Please hurry up and get to the problem," I thought to myself; yet he continued to elaborate.

"Well, on Friday, I bought her a wristwatch. It is a real nice one and I got it for a good price at the PX."

"Yes," I said slowly, the story now becoming much more interesting.

"Tonight," he continued, "I was wrapping up the watch and the Holy Spirit began to speak to me."

"Please go on!" I said, my heart

beginning to pound louder in my chest. Could this be my answer? Could this be JEHOVAH-JIREH at work for me?

"This is my problem: The Holy Spirit spoke to me to give the watch to Pastor Cho, but I know that you are a bachelor and don't need a girl's watch. You could only use a man's watch. What can I do?"

After I explained my story, the man got so excited, he began to dance around my office. "God really used me! God really used me!" he repeated over and over again. Both of us rejoiced as again God made provision in a way that I could have never imagined.

Since that time till this day, God has never failed me. He has allowed me to build the largest church in the history of this world, and He has miraculously provided every step of the way. He is not only the Provider for Abraham and Pastor Cho, but He is a Provider for you too!

God always meets our need out of His abundance. His abundant resources are not external, but are naturally based within His character and nature.

He is a Provider naturally, He just does not provide. Because by nature God is a God of provision, He is called JEHOVAH-JIREH.

If you can accept this, then you are on your way to seeing your needs met. Look at your need as an opportunity of seeing the Lord provide. Don't look at your need as a dead-end of opportunity —see it as the starting point of getting to know the Provider himself. He is able to meet your need, but He is looking to see if you will trust Him.

Won't you trust Him to meet your need?

If your need is healing, then please continue to read, because God is called, JEHOVAH-RAPHA.

JEHOVAH RAPHA: I AM GOD THAT HEALETH

We are living in an age of scientific and technological advancement unprecedented in the history of man. This day has seen the greatest discoveries in medicine; yet one fact still prevails—men and women are still sick. Insurance companies are charging larger premiums than ever before. Medical costs have become so expensive that people live in fear of getting sick lest their entire savings be wiped out by a hospital stay.

We also have people living longer than ever before. Older people live with the fear that they will become disabled and will have to be placed in a home or hospital to live their remaining lives in misery.

The need is as great today for healing as ever before. What is the answer for this staggering problem of sickness and disease? The answer is JEHOVAH-RAPHA.

As in the case with all of the names which manifest God's character and nature, this name of special provision was revealed to Israel during a time of need, as seen in Exodus 15:22. The story shows Israel traveling out into the Wilderness of Shur at the direction of Moses, and after three days in the hot desert, they could find no water. The greatest physical need that we have is water. A man can fast from food for many days, but he always needs water.

Israel began to complain about their circumstance, but soon they came upon a large pool of water, Marah (bitterness). As the name indicates, the water at this pool was bitter and was therefore undrinkable.

Moses was stuck. As the leader he could direct the people to go where God showed him, but then he had to take all of the criticism when things went wrong. However, Moses had learned to trust in God and instead of worrying, he prayed and asked God to show him what to do.

God revealed a tree nearby and asked him to do a strange thing. He took a portion of the tree and cast it into the bitter pool of water. After the tree settled on the waters, something happened. The water became sweet and was able to be consumed by the three million people and all of the animals that were with them. It was at this time that God revealed His name and provision to Israel. God said, "If thou wilt diligently hearken to the voice of the Lord thy God, and wilt do that which is right in His sight, and will give ear to His commandments, and keep all His statutes, I will put none of these diseases upon thee, which I have brought upon the Egyptians; for I am the Lord that healeth thee (JEHOVAH-RAPHA).

Notice that the Lord revealed himself as Healer not when the people needed healing but when the water needed healing. Also, God revealed himself as Healer within the context of a promise. He promised that He would keep the diseases that plagued Egypt from coming upon Israel. This means that God not only heals, but He can through His healing nature prevent disease from coming upon us as well. There is "preventative healing."

God is the same. His Son, Jesus Christ is the same. He never changes. The God who provided both actual and preventative healing to Israel is the same God who is able to meet our physical needs as well.

The reason for God revealing himself

as the Healer when the water was healed is because God meets and heals all of our diseases. Water was an integral part of Israel's consciousness: several of the plagues which plagued Egypt were shown on the water, and Israel's deliverance came through the opening of the Red Sea. This story takes on greater significance as we see the most important event in the human drama of history take place—the Cross. Jesus was crucified on a tree to bring deliverance to the human race. The tree was placed in the water to bring healing; so also the bitterness of human existence was healed because of the tree. When Christ was crucified, water and blood flowed from His side. All that we needed was in Christ at the Cross. As the Roman soldier, who pierced Christ found out, water and blood was the source of total and complete deliverance. We are saved because of the shed blood of Jesus Christ. That blood is still at work today. The Bible says that if we confess our sins, He is faithful and just to forgive us our sins and to cleanse us from all unrighteousness. That blood can cleanse us today.

We are also cleansed by the washing of the water of the Word of God. That powerful and sharp Word of God can go right to our souls and purify our thinking. Our thinking affects our bodies; therefore the water of the Word of God also is a healing agent. The blood and the water are very important symbols showing us the total and complete work of healing, which Christ is able to perform to all those that trust Him.

As agents in the hands of God, the healing that the blood and water bring not only gives us miraculous healing for our souls, minds and bodies, but it also prevents sickness by keeping us clean. We learn from medicine that much of our sickness today comes from negative thinking. According to recent medical studies, psychosomatic syndromes cause up to eighty percent of all sickness, and these figures are considered conservative. The fact is that the power of God can cause our thinking life to be so positive that we can have preventative healing. That is, we can be kept from diseases that could most likely come upon us by having His power at work within us, killing foreign objects that enter our bodies without our knowledge.

THE MINISTRY OF CHRIST

Our Lord spent two-thirds of His earthly ministry healing the sick, casting out demons and performing miracles. He not only performed healings, but also gave the disciples authority to do the same thing. Just before His ascension into heaven, He commanded us to follow His example. Our church is known throughout the entire country as a place where people can find help for their needs. When people get sick, even non-Christians know that in our church there exists a hope for receiving healing.

Some preachers teach that healing was a gift that Christ commanded the disciples to use until the time that the Bible was completed. Now that we live in a different age which does not require us to perform miracles, they say that the days of miracles are over, because we live in a civilized world. When I hear this kind of talk, I wonder whether these people ever read the newspaper or watch television. If the world is so civilized, then why is it that murderers and rapists run through the streets of our cities performing their horrible acts of violence? Why is it that so many people today are afraid to leave their homes at night and so many live behind bars of security? No! The world is not more civilized. The world is in more need for the miraculous power of God than ever before.

With 300,000-plus members in our church, I have literally thousands of stories of God's miracle-working power, too many to include in this book. But suffice it to say that we have seen God do what is physically impossible. This does not mean that we do not believe in medicine. Yes, God uses doctors. In fact, we have many prominent doctors in our congregation. Yet they are the first to tell you that medicine is not a science, but an art. That is, a doctor can only do his best and then he must trust in the recuperative power of the patient's body for the healing to take place.

In the latter part of the twentieth century, we need to know God as JEHOVAH-RAPHA.

JEHOVAH NISSI: JEHOVAH THE VICTORIOUS BANNER

As in every other revelation of God's nature manifested in His name, JEHOVAH-NISSI was revealed to Moses during a time of need. Exodus 17 shows us what happened. Let us look at it!

Moses had led Israel out of the Wilderness of Sin into the plains of Rephedim. Normally this area was well watered; however, all of the wells were dry when Israel arrived. The people began to complain to Moses and asked, "Why did you bring us to this place?" Being concerned for his very life because the people were ready to stone him, Moses again had to go to God. God spoke to him to take the rod which he had used previously to open the waters and strike the rock in Horeb. Waters came from the rock and met the needs of the people. Yet that place was named Massah and Meribah because of the tempting of God through lack of faith.

Right after this the children of Amalek attacked Israel, probably wanting the precious water. Moses commanded Joshua to raise an army to combat Amalek, while he joined Aaron and Hur at the top of a nearby hill. As Moses lifted his hands, Joshua was able to use Israel's untrained army to defeat Amalek. Yet, Moses' hands became heavy with fatigue, so Aaron and Hur had to support his hands until evening. In this way, Israel won a total victory over Amalek. Moses then built an altar to God at that place and called it: JEHOVAH-NISSI (The Lord Is My Banner).

Paul shows us that our wrestling match is not with flesh and blood, but with the principalities and powers. Therefore, our battle is in the heavenlies. As long as we think that our battle is with other people, we are tempted to use carnal weapons for warfare. Yet when we realize that our battle is with spiritual forces that use people, then we turn to our spiritual resources, which are mighty to the pulling down of strongholds of the enemy. Intercessory prayer is typified by Moses lifting up his hands to God. If we keep on praying and don't faint, prayer can change the circumstance. When Moses' hands came down, the enemy got the upper hand: When he was able to keep his hands up through the support of Aaron and Hur, the victory was won in time.

In 1969 God commanded me to build a church that would seat 10,000 people. That is the main auditorium that we are presently using until the new sanctuary is completed. All we had to begin with was two-thousand dollars. This was not enough money to buy the land in a new area of the city called Yoido. Yoido was being planned as the center of our nation's capital, similar to Capitol Hill in Washington D.C. As a flood had damaged the existing city, Dr. Il Suk Cha, then the vice-mayor of Seoul, was planning the area. When he flew over Yoido, he thought of Manhattan Island in New York and saw it as a place where the city of Seoul could grow without fear of flood damage.

On this island there was room made for one church. Dr. Cha, whose mother was a good member of my church, came to me and told me that the land could be made available to our church if I wanted it. What an opportunity! Yet our resources did not match our opportunity.

I then went to the bank and bought the land on credit. As we began constructing the church, everything possible went wrong. First our currency was devalued, causing economic inflation and uncertainty. Then came the oil embargo and the price of oil skyrocketed. This hit us in Korea more than it affected the western industrial countries. The contractors that had begun building our church were desirous of stopping the whole project, because there was no way to judge the increasing cost of materials that would be used in our building.

People in our church began losing their jobs and our income fell. What could I do? We had no money and our bills were piling up on my desk. I said to myself, "I wish this whole building would just collapse around me."

However, during this time we had started a new project called "Prayer Mountain." Every day more and more people were going to this prayer retreat area to fast and pray, mainly for their pastor. One evening, when things could not get any worse, I joined the people to pray and fast. Suddenly I could sense a change in the atmosphere: God had come on the scene. We all began to thank God for the answer. With this an old woman came up to me and said, "Pastor, I am an old lady and have no material possessions. All I have in this world is these two chopsticks and this rice bowl. As I asked

God what I should do to help you, I could only think of these two material possessions. So I would like to give this to God to help you build our church. I can use a newspaper to place my rice in, and I can eat it with my hands." I began to weep, and with the tears running down my face I said, "Please, I can't take these items from you."

"No. I have to give something to Jesus who has saved me. Please take my rice bowl and chop sticks. I know it's not much, but it is all I have."

With this action of extreme sacrifice, a man in the back of the room said, "I want to buy those items for $1,000." Then others began to sacrifice. My wife and I sold our home and gave the money to the church. Miraculously, we were saved from sinking and our church was completed. In 1973 we hosted Billy Graham in our church, and then we were able to use our facilities for the Tenth World Pentecostal Conference.

Through intercession and sacrifice we got to know JEHOVAH-NISSI. He fought our battles, not only in the financial area, but in every area of our life and ministry. Under His banner we travel throughout the world in Church Growth International Conferences and Meetings. We have seen Him perform miracle after miracle. Truly, He is our Victorious Banner.

JEHOVAH-SHALOM— JEHOVAH GIVES PEACE

Judges, chapter 6, again shows Israel in great need. At this time they were under the oppressive hand of the Midianites. Yet God had a plan for deliverance. However, His deliverance did not come in a way in which Israel could have ever imagined. God chose a man—Gideon, from the least of the tribes—Manasseh. This young man was the least in his father's household. The Angel of the Lord appeared to him as he was secretly working, hiding from the enemy. When the Angel addressed him, he called him a mighty man of valor. Obviously, Gideon had manifested no perceivable valor; however, God calls those things which are not as if they were. He is able to see the end from the beginning.

Gideon tested the Angel by bringing an offering. The Angel touched the offering with his staff and the offering was consumed, proving that God had accepted the sacrifice. Then Gideon said to the Lord, "Alas, O Lord God! For I have seen the Angel of the Lord face-to-face." Then the Lord granted him peace. "Peace be with you; do not fear, you shall not die." Therefore, Gideon built an altar to God and called it, The Lord Is Peace: JEHOVAH-SHALOM.

Above anything the world needs, it needs peace. The world today is caught up in a fearful arms race. Nuclear weapons are increasingly becoming available to unstable governments. There are a number of hot wars taking place in every continent. Vietnam has troops fighting in Cambodia; Russia has troops fighting in Afghanistan; Iran is fighting Iraq—and this is only in our continent of Asia. There are wars being fought in Central America, Africa and South America. Man is desperately in search of lasting peace. Yet the only hope for peace is the Prince of Peace: Jesus Christ.

Not only are wars raging in the world, but there are great battles being fought today in men's hearts. People are searching for reality and they are going to psychologists and psychiatrists in record numbers.

What kind of peace does JEHOVAH-SHALOM bring? It is a peace that passes understanding. It is a peace that gives us internal stability in the midst of trouble. It is a peace that the world cannot know, for the world only experiences peace when there is a cessation of hostility. When the circumstances warrant, then men think they have peace. However, the kind of peace that we can know is the peace that comes through Jesus Christ. His peace endures, although we still may be in the thick of the battle. His peace comes from delivering us from all fear.

In every experience that can take away our peace we can ask a simple question, "What is the worst thing that can happen to me in this situation?" When we think of the answer in the light of Scriptures, we realize that nothing can separate us from the love of God that is in Christ Jesus. Not death, life or angels, principalities, powers, things present, or things to come can separate us from the love of God in Christ Jesus. Everything is working for our good. We can't lose, for Christ has won the final and complete victory. This peace is ours by faith in Christ Jesus our Lord.

A young woman from one of the wealthiest families in Korea was in the hospital suffering from severe burns on her body. One of the ministers in our church paid her a visit. She regained consciousness long enough to say to our minister, "Please tell the world that money does not bring peace. I am from a very wealthy family. I have had everything money could buy. But right now, the only peace I have is an internal peace which comes only through Jesus Christ."

Another important aspect of the

peace that comes through Jesus Christ is that it is not temporary. The peace that Christ gives to us is an everlasting peace, which means that our eternity is secure in the God who is peace: JEHOVAH-SHALOM.

JEHOVAH RAAH— JEHOVAH IS THE GOOD SHEPHERD

Probably the best known Psalm is the 23rd Psalm. In this beautiful verse, David reveals the Lord as the Good Shepherd. The reason that the Lord is a good shepherd is that we can have complete and total confidence in His intentions and ability to take care of us as His sheep.

A shepherd does several things for His sheep:

1. He protects them.

Our Lord protects us from all of our enemies. We do not have to fight our battles, because He fights our battles for us.

2. He lays down His life for His sheep.

A bad shepherd does not have the kind of love that is willing to sacrifice anything for his sheep. Yet our Lord is a Good Shepherd in that He gave His life on Calvary for us. Because of this ultimate sacrifice, we are saved.

3. He leads them into green pastures.

Our Lord, the Good Shepherd, takes care of all of our needs and brings us into prosperity in those things which we do. It is not God's will that we fail, but it is God's will that we prosper and be in health even as our soul prospers.

4. He restores our souls.

The benefits of following our Shepherd is not only a once and for all experience, but it is a continual process of restoration. He renews our minds, our spirits and our bodies.

JEHOVAH-TSIDKEENU— JEHOVAH THE RIGHTEOUS

As the God of provision, every time His people were in need, the Lord made the provision with himself. For all of God's goodness comes naturally from His nature. His names, therefore, reveal His nature. So too with JEHOVAH-TSIDKEENU.

In the 23rd chapter of Jeremiah, God rebukes the bad shepherds that had led Israel. They had fleeced the sheep without restoring the sheep. They were only concerned about their needs and not the needs of the people. However, the situation was not without hope: God would provide the answer. He would raise up a shepherd, who would be called David. We understand that God was referring to the son of David: The Lord and Savior, Jesus Christ, not the natural king, David.

In the day that God would raise up the Good Shepherd, they would no longer have to remember God as the God that had led them out of Egypt.

This was the distant past, and Israel had a short memory. No. They were to refer to Him as: JEHOVAH-TSIDKEENU: the Lord who is righteous would be our righteousness.

From the first act of disobedience by our natural father, Adam, man has been plagued by sin. Sin has caused us to live way beneath our capacity. Yet God came himself in Jesus Christ and became the last Adam. Now we are the heirs of a new nature. Our new nature is no longer bound to sin, but our new nature is geared to obedience. We no longer have to live under the condemnation which comes from our old lives, but we are new creatures in Christ Jesus. We have been set free from condemnation and are free to obey God's Law. Yet, we do not have to depend on our righteousness which comes from our works: our righteousness is His and it is imputed to us by faith. Christ became sin for us, who had never known sin, so that we might become the righteousness of God in Him. The solution to the sin question was not dealt with by something that we did. God dealt with the sin question by paying the price for our unrighteousness with His dear Son. Now the debt has been paid once and for all. The whole world can take advantage of this great work accomplished at Calvary by accepting Jesus Christ as their Savior.

The righteousness that is imputed to us (that is, it is given to us without our earning it) is total and complete. When we receive Jesus Christ as our personal Savior, we are totally delivered from our sin and it is as if we had never sinned.

Hallelujah, what a Savior!

JEHOVAH-SAMMAH— JEHOVAH WHO IS WITH YOU ALWAYS

In Ezekiel 48 we see a very important prophecy regarding a city set aside for the Lord. In verse 9 Ezekiel says, "The district that you shall set apart for the Lord shall be 25,000 cubits in length and 10,000 in width." Only the priests would live in this city and the Lord would have a sanctuary in the middle of it. The Lord gives very specific instructions regarding this city, and the last verse is most specific. Verse 35, the last verse in the chapter, as well as the last verse in the entire Book of Ezekiel, is most specific: God said, "and the name of the city from that day shall be: The Lord is THERE: JEHOVAH-SAMMAH."

The city of God is the church of Jesus Christ. Christ dwells within His people. It is a holy city set apart from the world, and it is the place where He has chosen to dwell. God has chosen to manifest His greatness to the world, through the Church of Jesus Christ. However, the Lord not only dwells in the universal Church, but He specifically dwells in the Church of Jesus Christ individually.

In 1958, when I started my first church, a farmer's wife came to me. She was very humble and sincere. Worried and concerned, she sought for words to express her heart to me: "Pastor," she began, "let me know the address of God. You know, when I was Buddhist, I would go to the Buddhist temple and I would speak to Buddha. Now that I am a Christian, I don't see our Lord. So I must know His address. What is God's address? Since you are His servant and our pastor, you must surely know!"

Shocked at the question and not knowing exactly how to answer her, I simply replied, "I will let you know God's address soon." Then, I began to pray and think to myself, "God lives in heaven. But, wait a minute! Where is heaven? Well, if heaven is above me in the sky, then what about the people that live in Australia? Their sky is in the opposite direction as my sky." So I decided to look in the Scriptures.

In Genesis, when God created all things, Adam and Eve lived in the Garden of Eden. Alas, but the Garden of Eden is no longer. God moved into a tabernacle that Moses built, but that tabernacle was destroyed. Later, God moved into a temple built by Solomon; but every one of the temples was destroyed. Jesus certainly was God made flesh and dwelling among us on earth. Yet after Christ's resurrection, He ascended to heaven.

As I was praying, the Holy Spirit began to illuminate my young mind. Yes, Jesus ascended into heaven, but He sent the HOLY SPIRIT. That Holy Spirit is God dwelling in every believer. Therefore, the address of God is the address of every believer in the world. For God does not dwell in temples made with hands, but He dwells in the hearts of them that love Him.

I couldn't wait until Sunday morning. Word had gotten around that the pastor of the church was going to give God's address and the people were very curious.

"This morning, I am going to give you God's address," I said, looking at the people taking out their pencils and papers. They were about to begin writing when I spoke, "God's address is in you! Yes, you are the address of God! If the world wants to see God, they must look at you, because God has chosen you as the temple of the Holy

71

Ghost!" How happy everyone was. They suddenly realized that each one of us is the temple of the Holy Spirit. God is always with us, even to the end of this world.

Do you sometimes wonder whether anyone is concerned about your needs and problems? Well, you can know for sure that God is the answer to each one of our needs. He meets every need with himself. God is our answer. We must learn how to trust our God in every circumstance and situation.

Spurgeon was struck by the verse, "Look unto me and be ye saved." We too must learn to look to God for every single one of our needs. In this way, we can find that eternal answer within our Eternal God.

AMEN!

4

The Four Things the World Needs to Know

There are four basic things that people everywhere in the world need to know. These things are not new, but they are very important. We can never allow ourselves to think that everything of importance must be new to us. Paul repeated the same thing in different ways, using different examples to the churches that he had founded and encouraged.

In fact, in order for us to understand these four basic things that we need to know, we are going to look at the Apostle to the Gentiles, the Apostle Paul:

WHO WAS THE APOSTLE PAUL?

The Apostle Paul was not always a Christian. He grew up as a Jew in a town called Tarsus. Tarsus was an industrious city in the area known as Cilicia in what is now Turkey. The town was about twelve miles from the Mediterranean Sea on the banks of a lovely river. When the Romans conquered that area, about 64 B.C., they formed a community, Tarsus, where the governor lived.

At that time, Rome allowed a great deal of autonomy, especially in religious matters. This is why Paul was able to cast Christians into prison and beat some severely. He persecuted the saints from an early age, believing the new sect of Christianity to be revolutionary and dangerous. He had the responsibility of holding the coats of the men that stoned Stephen, the first Christian martyr. He was on his way to Damascus when he had an experience which would change his life dramatically. The Lord Jesus Christ appeared to Paul in a vision. Yet the others traveling with him only saw a bright light. He also heard the voice of Christ. The experience so changed him that he immediately wanted to use his energies to serve the same Lord that he had previously persecuted.

GOD PREPARES
THE VESSEL

God prepares the vessel before He uses it. Paul had been the only Jewish follower of Christ called to be an apostle, who had an extensive knowledge of the Gentiles. Being a Roman citizen, having been educated in the ways of Rome, and knowing the philosophies of the Greeks, Paul was specially prepared to reach the Gentile world for Christ.

The Holy Spirit had been at work in Paul ever since he saw Stephen stoned. Jesus told him, "It's hard to fight against the goads." A goad is a long stick with a sharp pointed end that sheep herders use to prod animals to move. Therefore, the Holy Spirit had been prodding Paul, and he reacted by persecutions.

When Paul was converted, he used the same natural zeal that caused him to persecute the church in building the church. Paul also showed a pragmaticism which was most likely acquired from having to deal with Gentiles in his home city of Tarsus. That is, when necessary, he used the fact that he was freeborn, to get out of trouble: he used the fact that he was a Roman citizen and also used the fact that he was a respected member of the Jewish religious class when he combated the Jews who tried to undermine his ministry.

Having his horizons expanded by his family and class, he was able to use that expanded vision to dream about spreading the gospel beyond the known reaches of the world. When writing to the Romans, he stated that he would visit them on the way to Spain, which was the Western frontier of the Roman Empire (Romans 15:24). Although he never got to Spain, he did go to Rome. He arrived in Rome on a free one-way ticket—in chains—but he did get there.

It seems that God uses a man or woman in a way that is natural to their previous circumstances. Daniel, a political leader in the Medo-Persian Empire, was able to see prophetic dreams and visions of Israel's political future. He dreamed concerning empires that would rise and fall. His natural capacity to think in political terms was used by God to give a clear and unmistakable view of God's people's future through the entire Roman Empire. So Paul, a man trained in travel, language, custom and thinking of the entire Roman Empire, was used by God to blaze the trail of the church to areas unthinkable to the apostles in Jerusalem.

GOD PREPARES THE AREA

Natural circumstances are to be used by the church to spread the Gospel of Jesus Christ. The relative safety brought about by Roman conquest resulting in the "Pax Romana" gave the messengers of the gospel the ability to travel and speak to many different people, without the problems other areas of the world had. Roads were built by Rome for military purposes, but were in reality vchicles for the propagation of the faith.

Syria in the east controlled Israel as part of the split of the empire founded by Alexander the Great. Yet, one of the successors, Attalus of Pergamum, after realizing the inevitability of Roman conquest, bequeathed his kingdom to Rome in 133 B.C. This gave Rome a large area without having to fight for it. It also was the reason why Rome was moderate in its dealings with the people of the area. Since Rome had shown its ruthlessness in totally destroying Carthage in 146 B.C., Israel was saved from a similar fate by this turn of history.

Not only the territory was prepared before the gospel of Christ was spread, but God also prepared the vehicle of communication. Although Rome had the military power, the Greeks had the culture. Therefore, the Greek language spread throughout the Roman Empire as the language of the educated. This caused the apostles to be able to communicate the gospel in the language of the people. Paul, who was able to speak and write the Greek language very well, was able to be heard even in sophisticated Athens. Although we read that the Athenians rejected Paul's story of the Resurrection, we never hear them criticize his Greek. The Greek language was also used by the evangelists and apostles to write the New Testament. Because the marketplace Greek was used (koine'), these scrolls could be read by everyone, not just scholars.

With this historical understanding, let us turn to our Scripture: Acts 16:6-10. Here we see *Paul's Call in the Night*, and from this point we shall also understand the *Four Things God Wants You to Know*.

The Council in Antioch took place around 49 A.D. Paul and Barnabas stayed in Antioch after the Council ruling which resolved the problems that caused much trouble with Gentile Christians: that is, that they need not be circumcised and follow the Law of Israel in order to be saved. Paul then proposed to revisit the churches in Galatia, to which Barnabas agreed. Yet Barnabas wanted to take John Mark, his nephew, along. Paul was against it, because John had proven to be unreliable on a previous journey. Paul took Silas the prophet and moved northward by land through Syria and Cilicia, where he had begun his apostolic ministry. Barnabas with John Mark went back to Cyprus, his home territory.

Traveling northward through the Cilician Gates, Paul reversed his former route and came first to Derbe and Lystra. At Lystra he found Timothy, the son of a Jewish mother and Greek father. After circumcising Timothy to protect him from Jewish accusation, Paul allowed him to join the team. However, Titus, a full-blooded Gentile, was not required to be circumcised (Gal. 2:3).

Now comes some very interesting verses. In verses 7 and 8, we see that they were forbidden by the Holy Spirit to preach either in Asia or Bithinia. Why?

The purpose of the journey was to tell the new Gentile churches the results of the Council's ruling: except for some points, they were free from the Jewish law; they were to abstain from food offered to idols, from fornication; from eating strangled animals and from eating blood.

If we look at a map detailing the area where Paul preached on his second missionary journey, we see the answer clearly. Asia is the province which had the roads to the south leading to the seaport of Ephesus. From Asia, Paul and his team could travel back to Antioch after fulfilling their mission of teaching the saints and setting them free from future problems with Jewish legalism. Yet God had another plan.

Bithinia, a province in the north, had the land route back to Antioch. Yet the Holy Spirit said no. It could be that the Holy Spirit was speaking through the prophet Silas (Acts 15:32). However, we are told that the Holy Spirit clearly revealed to Paul that these two areas were not to be traveled to. The only logical thing to do was to continue to travel forward. If God would not let him take a southern route or northern route, then he must travel straight ahead. He continued to move ahead until he got to the sea town of Troas. Troas was on the Aegean Sea and before Paul was Macedonia. Would the Holy Spirit direct him to travel across the sea and go to a land that was populated by few Jewish communities? Could he minister to a people who were so taken up by practices and customs which were totally foreign to Jews? These were the thoughts that most likely perplexed Paul as he lay on his bed at night.

At this nighttime of Paul's experience, God gave him a vision that was not only to revolutionize his life, but also changed the entire course of human history till this day.

The Christian faith began in the continent of Asia. In fact, all of the historical major religions of the world have begun in Asia. The gospel of Jesus Christ continued to be preached in Asia Minor until the point in time when Paul saw a vision of a Macedonian saying, "Come and help us." A Macedonian had a particular look which was very different from a resident of Asia Minor. He was a European. His dress was less conservative. He was clean shaven. He represented a lifestyle that was repugnant to the modesty of the East. Yet God wanted to reach Europe with the gospel of our Lord and Savior, Jesus Christ.

Also at Troas we suddenly notice that the author of the Acts of the Apostles, Luke, begins to say "we." Obviously Luke, a Greek doctor, also joined Paul in a team that would successfully reach the Gentile world. This team made up of Silas (a Jewish prophet) and Timothy (a half-Jew), joined by Titus (a full-blooded Greek), and now by Luke (a Greek doctor) would have been totally unacceptable to the conservative Palestinian areas.

But God had put a team together that would be able to reach the people of Europe.

Europe would preach the gospel throughout the world and settle the new continent of the Americas. And we in Korea received the gospel of Jesus Christ through American missionaries.

This new continent needed to know four things. These same four things are also vitally important to every creature under God's heaven. These four things are necessary for your eternal life. What four things does the world need to know?

1. THEY NEED TO KNOW A TOTAL AND COMPLETE SALVATION.

The whole world needs to know the fact that Jesus has purchased their salvation, if they would only receive it. The world until this day is lost in sin and ignorance of the life that is waiting for them in Jesus Christ.

The Four Things the World Needs to Know

I was asked by a young man a common question: "Pastor Cho, how could God be a loving God with all of the sickness, wars and misery in this world?" The young man had a barber shop nearby. I asked him to take a walk with me. Then, I showed him a man in the distance that was obviously down and out. His hair was uncombed, his clothes were ragged and his face had a tattered beard. I then asked him, "How can you be a barber and allow that man to walk around the streets of this city looking like that?"

Acting rather defensive, the barber responded, "How can I take responsibility for that man if he doesn't come into my shop to be taken care of? I have all of the equipment to clean him up, shave his beard and cut his hair, but he has to come into the shop."

"Well, God has provided the answer for all of men's needs in Christ. However, if they don't come into His storehouse of salvation, man has to continue in his plight of suffering." The young man quickly got the point.

All that we need to solve all of our

problems in this life is Jesus Christ. The bill has been paid already. But mankind is still walking around like the beggar I referred to, because he doesn't know the bill at the shop has been paid already. Mankind needs to be told that salvation has been purchased for him at Calvary: All he has to do is receive it.

Recently, while I was preaching in America, I heard a true and moving story. During the days of the Civil War, over one hundred years ago, the North was fighting the South in the United States. As happens in wars, soldiers were captured by both sides. A general from the North discovered a Southern officer that needed to be executed. The Southern captain was getting ready to face the terminal bullet from the Northern general's gun when something unusual happened. In the distance he heard shouts: "Please, sir, do not kill the captain! I will gladly take his place. We are from the same town and I have known him most of my life. The captain has a wife and children, but I have no one back home.

Please, kill me instead!" As the general looked at the young man that was standing in front of him, his heart was moved by the courage displayed. The Northern general granted permission, and the young soldier died in place of the captain.

After the war, the captain was released from prison and was free to go back home to his family. Getting involved in business and the raising of his children, the captain forgot about the sacrifice that was made for him years earlier.

Billy Sunday came into this small town in the South and held an evangelistic campaign. The former captain was asked to attend. Billy started telling the story of how Christ had died in our place that we might be saved. Jesus paid the price for our sins that we might be saved. With that, the memory of the young man came rushing back into his mind. "Jesus was like the man who willingly died for me so that I could be here right now," he thought to himself as tears filled his eyes. With that, he accepted Jesus Christ as his

Savior and began to live a faithful Christian life.

"All we like sheep have gone astray; we have turned everyone to his own way, and the Lord hath laid on him [Jesus Christ] the iniquity of us all" (Isa. 53:6). We all need to accept Jesus Christ as Savior, or that sacrifice made for us almost two thousand years ago will be of little value to us, neither in this life nor in eternity. "If we confess our sins, He is faithful and just to forgive us our sins and to cleanse us from all unrighteousness" (1 John 1:9).

When Paul went to the new territory of Europe he first preached salvation through Christ. The Greeks were not serious about religion. Their gods had all of the human frailties that they had. Their gods were obviously a creation of their own minds. They had so many gods, because they did not want to displease any of them. If someone came with a new god, they just accepted it and added it to their already large list. Yet Paul preached a new message: There is only one God. This in itself was not new: Zoroaster had preached the Only Wise God for many years. This was the religion of the Medo-Persian Empire. What was new was that this one God had come in the person of His Son, Jesus Christ. Christ had lived a sinless life on this earth. He had died and was buried and then was resurrected on the third day.

How could Gentile Greeks accept this totally new concept of religion? Paul proved the power of God by healing the sick and casting out demons.

2. THEY NEED TO KNOW HEALING

Not long ago, I was in Switzerland in a healing campaign. After teaching the Word of God, the Holy Spirit prompted me to pray for the sick. The people responded to the call for healing by the hundreds. The Holy Spirit again spoke to my heart more specifically: "Tell the people that someone who is in a wheelchair is going to be healed!"

"Dear Father, how can I say that?" I

responded, after looking around and noticing an elderly lady in a wheelchair not too far from the platform. However, the Holy Spirit continued to speak to me to pronounce the healing to the wheelchair patient. Knowing that the Holy Spirit never changes His mind, I could no longer resist. Still shaking from the knowledge that the consequences of a failure in this area would bring disastrous consequences regarding my credibility, I obeyed. Yet, not obeying completely, I gave myself the latitude of time by saying, "Someone is going to be healed that is sitting in a wheelchair during this conference!"

After completing my ministry, I resolved to be as specific in my obedience as the Holy Spirit had been in His command. I then stepped down from the platform and looked right at the woman. Her eyes had a look of expectancy as I said directly to her, "God has healed you." I then returned to the platform. Then suddenly I heard a noise in the general area where I had just been. I focused my attention there and noticed that people were clapping happily. The lady and her husband were both pushing the wheelchair towards their automobile and people were rejoicing all of the way. God had healed her!

God's Holy Word says: "If thou wilt diligently hearken to the voice of the Lord thy God, and wilt do that which is right in His eyes, and wilt give ear to His commandments, and keep all of His statutes, I will put none of these diseases upon thee, which I have brought upon the Egyptians: for I am the Lord that healeth thee" (Exod. 15:26). God is a God that heals!

Twenty-five years ago I was a dying man. No doctor could give me any hope. I was supposed to die in three months. I did not know Jesus Christ as my Savior, so every day I was chanting to Lord Buddha, vomiting blood. One day a young lady brought me a Bible and told me about the love of God expressed through Jesus Christ. When I accepted Jesus Christ as my Savior, this same Jesus came into my heart. I was not only saved, but I was also healed of tuberculosis. I later went to Bible college and became a minister of the gospel of Jesus Christ.

Not long ago I was at our Wednesday night service. After leaving the platform, I headed directly towards my office. As usual, there was a long line of people waiting for me to pray for them. In this group of people was a young boy who had a cancer in his abdomen the size of a baseball. As I looked at that child who was still too young to be able to speak and saw the look of desperation in his eyes, my heart melted with compassion. The Holy Spirit came upon me as I strongly rebuked the cancer and prayed for his complete healing. Then I felt a peace come over my heart as I knew that God had heard and answered my prayer.

Several months later some people came toward me as I was in our television studio making teaching tapes for our international television ministry. I then noticed that these were the boy's parents and their faces reflected the joy that they felt. They then started to share the amazing testimony of their child's complete healing. Everyone rejoiced as the child came to me and threw his arms around my neck and began to smile.

The Bible teaches us that Satan has come to "rob and kill, and to destroy"; "I am come," Jesus said, "that they might have life, and that they might have it more abundantly" (John 10:10). You and I are able to claim our healing because Jesus Christ purchased it at the Cross.

Yet, after Paul prayed for the sick and cast out the demons, the Macedonians still needed to know how to live victoriously.

3. THEY NEED TO KNOW HOW TO LIVE.

Jesus Christ did not come to teach us how to die, but He came to teach us how to live. His death gives us life. Our death to sin and disobedience brings Him joy.

What kind of life does Christ want us to live? He desires that we live abundantly. He wants us to be healthy: spirit, soul and body.

The people of Europe did not know how to live before the coming of Jesus Christ to their continent in the persons of Paul and his team. The whole continent was lost in darkness and sin. The Greeks had philosophy and science. They were the first to discover the political system of democracy. Yet with all of their observations and knowledge, their hearts were darkened by sin. The evils of lust, homosexuality and greed dominated much of the culture. They worshiped themselves. Their sculpture pictured the perfect man, not the perfect God. Their philosophy tried to understand the universe, but was not able to have an understanding of its beginnings. Their science attempted to know the world, but their hearts were lost to the sickness of this world. Only Jesus could set them free. The qualities of hard work and honesty were unknown in the European culture of Paul's day. What made the difference? The preaching of the gospel of Jesus Christ. Prosperity has come to the European cultures, not because of a natural propensity toward hard work and honesty. No. It has come because of the blessings which always accompany the gospel of Christ: a change in the self-image of the people.

Twenty years ago, our people in Korea were very poor. The aftermath of the war left poverty and misery everywhere. We were all struggling to rise above the destruction and hope-lessness that was on every hand. When I came to church, most of the people were starved. I had no rice to give them. Winter time in Korea was very cold, and few people had enough warm clothes to keep their bodies warm. I began preaching the gospel of Jesus Christ in this economic condition.

Some criticized me by saying, "You can't eat this book called the Bible. This gospel of Jesus Christ cannot warm your house during winter nights. What good is it?"

But I responded, "This gospel can change your thinking life. It can change your self-image. It can cause you to know the fact that you are special to

God and therefore important. Once your attitude changes, your circumstances will also change."

Soon, people started to listen to the good news that God could change their circumstances. He can cause you to know how to live, and live more abundantly. As they began to move out into a faith life, miracles started to happen. And then, they began to prosper and be successful. Their positive "can do" attitude came as a direct result of the preaching of the gospel of Jesus Christ.

The Bible says: "My God shall supply all of your needs according to His riches in glory by Christ Jesus" (Phil. 4:19). This promise is for the here and now. This promise is very practical. This promise is not conditional; it is definite. God does not tell us that He *might* provide our needs. No! He *shall* provide for all of our needs. He does this from the well of His eternal resources in Christ Jesus, for in Christ lies all of the treasures. In Him the fullness of the Godhead dwells bodily. He is our resource in God. We cannot have a need that God is not responsible to meet.

From the seeds of poverty, we have seen with our own eyes God's ability to provide for our needs and give us the ability to build the largest church in the world. God has done this by changing our way of thinking and, in turn, our way of living.

I am concerned when minorities in countries like America believe that they are poor and deserving of hand-outs. This will only entrap them in the clutches of inferiority. The only way to be set free from poverty is to know that we are heirs of God's eternal resources in Christ.

We Koreans were under Japanese domination for years. We lost our names, the Japanese giving us their names. We almost lost our language and culture, the Japanese forcing us not to speak or write in Korean and destroying our rich literature. Yet by the help of God we have survived to forgive them and now have an extensive ministry in Japan.

Last year we were in the third poorest country in the world. Sri Lanka (Ceylon) has a per capita income of thirty dollars per month. They have been colonized by European countries for over four-hundred years. Understandably, they have had a poor self-image. Having gained their independence from Britain, they tried Communism, but that only made the situation worse. This almost totally Buddhist country has had poverty for so long that they almost believed that it was their natural state.

We had a Church Growth International Conference there in which we invited leaders from all of the churches. Roman Catholics, Anglicans, Lutherans, Methodist, Baptists and Pentecostals joined leaders from all other Christian churches to bring a total of over five-hundred attending the conference.

Our first dinner meeting saw people that were mostly non-Christian attending. In fact, we had the leader of the Communist party at the banquet. We also had men and women who wore

Buddhist garments. I preached to them the same, simple gospel that I would preach in our church. I made it clear to them that I personally knew the devastation of poverty. They listened and responded. After we closed the meetings, we saw hundreds accept Jesus Christ as their personal Lord and Savior. Jesus is the same yesterday, today and forever!

What is the answer to all of the poverty and misery in this world? Men must have a change in thinking. This will produce a change in living that will change their material circumstances. What can produce this change? The same message that Paul preached in Macedonia.

What caused European society to change over a period of time? What is causing change in our Korean society today? This change is only coming about by a change in the heart brought about by the gospel of Jesus Christ, which is the power of God.

4. THEY NEED TO KNOW THAT THEY WILL BE WITH JESUS CHRIST FOR ALL OF ETERNITY.

Last year, over one thousand Americans were polled in California and asked, "What do you fear most?" Over eighty-two percent of those polled said that they feared death above everything else. If someone could find the secret to living forever, most people would give up everything else to continue to live beyond their normal life spans.

Death is no respecter of persons, it affects the rich as it affects the poor. It catches up with the genius as quickly as the idiot. It takes the powerful as quickly as those that have no power. Therefore, death is feared by all.

The body has built within itself defense mechanisms to protect itself from danger. Reflexes are part of them and spring into action when something is thrown at you, even before you think about it. Yet the body eventually falls prey to death.

However, Jesus Christ conquered death at Calvary. Now we can join with Paul and say, "Death is swallowed up in victory. O death, where is thy sting? O grave, where is thy victory?" (1 Cor. 15:55). Although Paul was quoting from Hosea 13:14, he knew this truth experientially.

Christ died and destroyed the power of death. Now we are set free. Yet Christians still die. Yes. But we really live forever, for death is no longer a termination, but a transition: to be absent in the body is to be present with the Lord.

In the Gospel according to John, Jesus said, "Let not your heart be troubled!" What was the cause of the trouble? Jesus goes on to reveal that He would prepare a place for us that "where He is, so there we would be also" (John 14).

Approximately fifteen years ago, in a vision, I went into the third heaven and was there for about three hours. I met one missionary whom I had known and loved on this earth as we worked for God. In heaven he was so happy and

101

full of life and health. As I sat down with him, we talked about the days when we had worked for God. Everything in heaven was beautiful beyond description. Music that was beyond anything that I had experienced before filled the atmosphere. The one prevailing thing that I was aware of was the glorious presence of the Lord.

I was so happy being there that I did not want to return to this earth. But I heard the voice of God tell me, "You must go back and preach this gospel to all people!"

Yes, I know very well how real heaven is. I also know that if heaven is that real, hell must be just as real as well.

Paul gave the new people of Europe the first glimpse of the hope that purifies us by preaching the gospel of Jesus Christ. By accepting this Lord and Savior, they would be able to escape the entrapment of old age: the fear of death. They would be able to live productively, knowing that our works on this planet are going to be judged in heaven. What we become, we become for eternity. There is nothing wasted, except by sin.

Therefore, it behooves us to listen to the Gospel of Jesus Christ and be saved. Once we are saved, our whole life will be able to fall into line.

The Lord not only saves, but He also heals and sets free from all bondages. He wants us to live happy, healthy and productive lives. He also wants us to know that this life is not all. We are only pilgrims in this world. Our eternity is secure because He lives. Yes. Because He lives, we shall live also.

When the people first heard this message of Christ in Macedonia, many doubted, but many were saved. Later, the Church grew and flourished in Europe. And while much of the Church disappeared in Asia Minor (that area being taken over by the Moslems in later times), the Church has grown in the West. From the West we have received the gospel back here in the East. Now the largest church in the world is not in Europe or in America, it is here in the Orient.

Yet it is our responsibility to take the gospel to the ends of the earth until Jesus comes.

We cannot spare anything in bringing this matchless gospel to all of the world. Because when this gospel is preached in all of the world as a witness to all nations, the end shall come.

How I desire to see our Lord Jesus return! Don't you?

How can we hasten His return? By being obedient to reach out to the ends of the world with this message that Jesus saves, heals, teaches how to live and will bring us to live with Him for all eternity in heaven.

5

Peter Looked at the Wind and Began to Sink

Every child of God wants to have strong and profound faith. But faith is not acquired by accident. It comes to us through the Holy Spirit. In order for faith to grow and become strong it must go through certain tests.

Jesus showed His disciples the power of faith in the desert of Bethsaida when he fed over five thousand people with only five loaves and two fishes. Through this miracle the disciples saw that Jesus was truly God, that He solves human problems and loves people. They also realized, not in theory, but in practice, that the words of Jesus have power.

The Leap of Faith

Now that the disciples believed in Him, Jesus wanted to test their faith to see whether it was alive or not.

JESUS LET THE DISCIPLES GO AHEAD OF HIM TO THE OTHER SIDE

After Jesus performed the miracle in the desert of Bethsaida, He asked His disciples to go ahead of Him to the other side of the sea by boat. He usually stayed with the disciples, but this time He sent them on ahead.

When the disciples were gone, Jesus dispersed the crowd and went to the mountain to pray alone. Do you know what He prayed for? Perhaps He prayed that the disciples would pass the test He was going to put them through. Even today Jesus prays that we will pass the tests of our faith.

God allows us to go through certain tests so that our faith can grow stronger. Great faith is the result of severe testing. It is not easy to pass the tests of faith.

Peter Looked at the Wind

When we go through testing we feel lonely. When Jesus tested His disciples He let them go on alone. He didn't stay with them. When our faith is being tested we feel like the world has deserted us. We suffer pain and agony in our heart.

And that is not all. When we are being tested we feel as though we were passing through a night of utter darkness. The disciples were tested in the open sea of Galilee in utter darkness. At the time our faith is going to be tested, we do not know what the future holds for us. Our personal life, and the lives of our family look precarious and unstable. It doesn't seem like our faith is working at all.

The testing of our faith also brings stormy winds. The Bible says, "The boat by this time was many stadia away from the land, battered by the waves; for the wind was contrary" (Matt. 14:24).

When our faith is being tested, circumstances become very unfavorable toward us. A strong wind brings waves of despair and difficulty. Being tested tires us out. The disciples were struck by the stormy wind and high waves at the "fourth watch" of the night.

The fourth watch in modern terms is two o'clock in the morning. Robbers break into houses at this time, taking advantage of this wee hour of the morning. The most difficult hours for a sentry are the early morning hours. That is why scouts penetrate enemy territory around two in the morning. People are usually fast asleep at 2 A.M. It was at this hour that Jesus tested the disciples' faith.

Many people complain and say, "Why am I having such terrible troubles at this time?" The Lord wants us to go through a series of tests so that our faith may become strong. When we successfully pass the tests of faith, God is pleased to richly bless us. He wants us to be prosperous in all things and to be in good health even as our soul prospers.

JESUS CAME TO THE DISCIPLES WALKING UPON THE WATER

At the point when the test of our faith is at its peak, Jesus comes to us. The Scripture says, "In the fourth watch of the night, He came to them, walking upon the sea" (Matt. 14:25). When we face the wind and the waves we think Jesus has left us, but actually the winds and the waves are the way He comes to us. The Bible says, "The Lord sits upon the flood" (Ps. 29:10).

When there are winds and waves in our lives, we must remember that Jesus comes to us walking upon the waves. Jesus is our Helper. He solves our problems. In the desert of Bethsaida Jesus shows himself to be a God who solves people's problems.

Do you have troubles and problems in your life? I urge you to remember that in the midst of the wind and the waves, Jesus comes extending His hand to you.

The disciples of Jesus were troubled when they saw the wind and the waves.

They were also terrified when they saw Jesus walking on the water. Sailors in those days believed that if you saw a ghost at sea you would sink and perish. The disciples were really afraid when they saw Jesus. They completely forgot the experience they had in the desert of Bethsaida.

Today liberal and neo-theologians do not believe in the miracles of Jesus. They do not preach that Jesus is a God who performs miracles. They denounce such ideas as Christian shamanism or superstition. They are like the disciples who thought Jesus was a ghost when they saw Him walking on the water.

In spite of the progress of modern science and the improvement of human technology, God still performs miracles which transcend our understanding. When we look at Jesus' birth and life, for instance, we see a life of miracles which the most sophisticated technologies of modern science can never duplicate.

Jesus raised the dead and even caused things to come into being from nothing. He is not a God of the past.

Peter Looked at the Wind

Jesus Christ is the same yesterday, today and forever. He is alive right now. He hears our prayers and solves our problems. He performs miracles for us.

If someone does not believe in the miracles of Jesus, they are in essence denying the very existence of God. Divine help is not available to someone like this. He or she will sink and drown when confronted with life's problems.

Today we see many miracles occurring in churches that are "alive." We see the lost being saved, the sick healed and demons cast out. When you see signs such as these, do not pass them off as ghosts. Accept them for what they are—accept miracles as miracles.

Jesus said to His disciples, "Take courage, it is I; do not be afraid." He showed them that He is a God of love. Jesus is still saying to us today, "I love you." I want you to be prosperous in all things and be in good health even as your soul prospers. It is I. Take courage. Do not be afraid. Do not look at the wind and the waves and the darkness."

It doesn't matter whether it is completely dark or not when you are with Jesus. You don't need to be afraid or doubtful. Even though the future may look dark and dismal, when Jesus is with you, your future is secure and solid.

Jesus said, "What man is there among you, when his son shall ask him for a loaf, will give him a stone? Or if he shall ask for a fish, he will not give him a snake, will he? If you then, being evil, know how to give good gifts to your children, how much more shall your Father who is in heaven give what is good to those who ask Him?" (Matt. 7:9-11).

Jesus tells the person who is groaning in the wind and waves of mental agony, "Take courage, it is I; do not be afraid." I want you to know that Jesus is a God who solves our problems, performs miracles and loves us individually.

PETER WAS COURAGEOUS

When Jesus appeared and said, "Take courage, it is I; do not be afraid,"

Peter Looked at the Wind

Peter said, "Lord, if it is you, command me to come to you on the water."

Out of all twelve of the disciples, only Peter responded to Jesus. Peter was looking at the Jesus who performed a miracles in the desert of Bethsaida, who fed thousands of people with five loaves and two fishes. He was looking at a Jesus who was walking on the water. Peter was convinced that Jesus was a God who performs miracles, solves problems and loves people. His faith was positive and productive. That is why he could say to the Lord, "If it is you, command me to come to you on the water."

Believers who are convinced that Jesus performs miracles, solves problems and loves us, can come boldly to the throne of God and entrust Him with every trouble they have. Though they see no material proof with their physical eyes, though they hear no voice with their physical ears and though they cannot touch something tangible with their physical hands, they know for sure they are dealing with a God who is alive and all powerful.

Jesus bore the cross in order to blot out the problems of sin, sickness, the curse and death. He bestowed on us the miracles of regeneration, divine healing, material blessing, the fullness of the Holy Spirit and the hope of His second coming.

Peter believed in Jesus and asked Him for words of power on which he could exercise his faith. He said, "Lord, command me to come to you on the water."

We are not to exercise blind faith. The Bible says, "Faith comes from hearing, and hearing by the Word of Christ" (Rom. 10:17). When Peter asked for an opportunity to exercise his faith, Jesus said, "Come." Peter ignored the circumstances around him and relied on the words of Jesus.

There were twelve disciples in the boat, but Jesus only told Peter to come. It is the same way today. God responds to those who cry out to Him. He gives eternal life to those who ask for salvation, healing to those who seek a cure, material blessing to those who ask for it. He never gives anything to those who ask nothing from Him. When we are bold in our requests, the Lord responds to our earnest call and says, "Come."

How do we know this is true? Because it is recorded in the Word of God. Read the Scriptures for yourself, from Genesis to Revelation. Then you can understand the promises of God and put them into practice by faith.

Jesus also gives us His words through our prayers. We must ask the Lord to give us His words. God will answer our prayer and grant specific words that we can apply in our individual lives. The Word of God never changes. Heaven may change and the earth may change, but God's Word never changes. We must not look at circumstances, but stand firm on the foundation of God's Word to us.

There are certain lessons we can learn from Peter's failure as well. The way we understand what happened to Peter may change our entire life. When Jesus said to Peter, "Come," Peter didn't look at the wind or the waves. He only looked at Jesus. He stood on the words of Jesus. Then he slowly stepped out of the boat and began walking on the water. A tremendous thing happened to Peter. His feet didn't sink into the water. He was walking on water as though he were walking on the ground. As long as he looked at Jesus and relied upon His words he had no fear. As a result he walked on the water.

But Matthew tells us that Peter saw the wind and was afraid. At that point he began to sink. He had turned his eyes from Jesus and looked at the wind and the waves instead. This caused negative thoughts to come into his heart. His mind began filling with doubt and fear and his feet began sinking into the water.

It's the same today. When we do not look in the right direction or do not think in the right way, we fall into despair and despondency. We lose courage in God's grace when we look and think in the wrong direction.

When God told Noah to build the ark He told him only to put windows in the ceiling of the ship. This was for the benefit of Noah's family. This way they would not be able to look at the circumstances around them. Noah and his family lived in the ark for more than a year, but they never saw what was happening around the ship. They could only look up through the window in the ceiling. They could remember God's words of promise and focus on Him.

A year later the ark rested on the top of Mt. Ararat and they safely left the ship. If Noah and his family had seen the world being destroyed by the flood, they would have been so overcome with shock that they would never have gotten out of the ship alive.

Negative thoughts and doubts bring fear and frustration. We cannot focus on God or stand on His Word when our minds are filled with negative thoughts. When we look only at the Lord and stand firmly on His Word, then we can live a victorious Christian life.

In order to experience God's grace, we must shut the door of our senses. When tests and troubles come, fear and doubt will fill our hearts if we rely on our senses. We must focus our attention on God and His promises, not on our senses or the circumstances around us. I pray that all of you will be able to live successfully and victoriously by applying this principles in your lives.

Jesus taught His disciples a precious lesson through the test in the sea of Galilee. He taught them what to see, hear and think. He showed them they must always think of Him as a God who performs miracles, solves problems and bestows love on us. It was a lesson which taught them to think positively and creatively.

Let me ask you a question. What do you see, hear and think? Do you see Jesus as someone who gives you eternal life, the fullness of the Holy Spirit, divine healing, material blessings and the hope of His second coming? No matter what difficult situation you face, focus on your good and gracious Father who takes care of you. Think on His promises. Don't allow doubt or fear to come into your heart. God is Alpha and Omega, the beginning and the end.

He caused even the dead to be raised up, and can make something out of nothing.

Our world is full of changes and emptiness. People are full of deceit and lies. But God is the same forever. His words are all true. When we stand firmly on this Rock of Ages, our faith will be strengthened and we will see, hear and think in the right way. The wind and waves of the world will not cause us to fall. We will have faith and victory in our Christian walk.

Peter looked at Jesus and relied on His word and he walked on water. But when he allowed negative thoughts to come into his mind, fear and doubt caused him to sink and begin to drown.

Success or failure in life depends on our heart attitude. The Bible says, "Watch over your heart with all diligence. For from it flow the springs of life" (Prov. 4:23). At this very moment, Jesus is waiting for you to have strong faith. Why don't you focus on Him who can solve your problems?

Think of His words of promise and proceed boldly to the throne of God expecting His rich blessing and victory to flow into your life!